# adultolescence

# adultolescence

## gabbie hanna

**Keywords**
PRESS

ATRIA

New York · London · Toronto · Sydney · New Delhi

ATRIA

An Imprint of Simon & Schuster, Inc.
1230 Avenue of the Americas
New York, NY 10020

First Keywords Press / Atria Paperback edition September 2017

Keywords Press / **ATRIA** PAPERBACK and colophons are trademarks of Simon & Schuster, Inc.

For information about special discounts for bulk purchases, please contact Simon & Schuster Special Sales at 1-866-506-1949 or business@simonandschuster.com.

The Simon & Schuster Speakers Bureau can bring authors to your live event. For more information or to book an event contact the Simon & Schuster Speakers Bureau at 1-866-248-3049 or visit our website at www.simonspeakers.com.

Manufactured in the United States of America

10   9   8   7   6   5   4   3   2

Library of Congress Cataloging-in-Publication Data

Names: Hanna, Gabbie, author.
Title: Adultolescence / Gabbie Hanna.
Description: First paperback edition. | New York CIty : Keywords Press, 2017
Identifiers: LCCN 2017033612 (print) | LCCN 2017028569 (ebook) | ISBN 9781501178337 (ebook) | ISBN 9781501178320 (softcover) | ISBN 9781501178337 (ebook)
Subjects: | BISAC: POETRY / American / General. | POETRY / General.
Classification: LCC PS3608.A71544 (print) | LCC PS3608.A71544 A6 2017 (ebook) | DDC 811/.6–dc23
LC record available at https://lccn.loc.gov/2017033612

ISBN 978-1-5011-7832-0
ISBN 978-1-5011-7833-7 (ebook)

for all the kids who grew up too fast,
all the adults who refuse to grow up,
and everyone who's both.

# ACKNOWLEDGMENTS

As much as I'd just love to take all the credit for this book, there are a lot of people who had a hand in making this dream come to life.

To Shane Dawson: Thank you for pushing me to stop putting this off and just start writing. You inspire and encourage me in so many ways. Mostly, thank you for putting me in touch with a great publishing team with a glowing recommendation. Real friends lie for each other.

To Jhanteigh Kupihea: Thank you for dealing with my anxiety, my unbearable pickiness, and my four-in-a-row-ten-word emails that I could have easily sent in one. Also, for constantly [trying to] calm my neuroticism. You are my editor and my therapist. You are my Edapist. Oh, and thanks for never making me say your last name out loud.

To Judith Curr: Thank you for believing in my vision, like, literally immediately. It was a hell of a lot faster than I did.

To Ariele Friedman: Thank you for doing publicist-y things that somehow tricked people into thinking I was somebody important-ish.

To my siblings: Cherisa, Monica, Cecilia, Genevieve, Madelynn, and Sammy. Thank you for being my siblings. I love you and stuff.

To everyone who I relentlessly sent slews of poems and drawings to over the past few months begging for opinions, encouragement, and validation. Thank you and I'm sorry.

To all of my supporters and followers: Thank you for standing by me through the years. You were there when I was sad-tweeting limericks at 5 a.m. and telling me to write a poetry book. You were the ones that were buying and supporting before it even came out. You are the reason for not only this book, but my entire existence. I am so overwhelmed with your love and I return it eleven-fold.

And lastly: To everyone who tore my heart out. I owe you one.

# AUTHOR NOTE

*this book was inspired by bo burnham*
*who was inspired by shel silverstein*
*so i suppose by the transitive property*
*this book is inspired by shel silverstein*
*which i'm cool with because he's dope.*

# UNEXPECTED

ladies and gentlemen,
come have a look!
here at last,
another youtuber book!
just what we needed!
someone to produce
the tangible ego of
a twenty-something douche.

# RECESS

jacob and emily sitting in a tree

K-I-S-S-I-N-G

first came love

then came marriage

then came a stale & empty life

as a result of the societal pressures

to wed which led

to a semi-public affair and a severe

case of alcoholism

mixed with mental illness

followed by a grueling 2-year divorce

that damaged the kids emotionally

and left everyone without

a sense of direction or self-worth

# O-POSITIVE

i donated blood today.

feels good to finally be somebody's type.

# ADVICE 14

when i was a kid my biggest fear was getting lost in
space & it turns out maybe i shouldnt have been so
stressed about that bc i dont have a spaceship so dont
make problems where there arent any

# BFF

Lonely's been my bestest friend
for as long as i remember.
he gets a little clingy,
especially mid-to-late december.
but Lonely's alway been there
every single time i've cried.
through all the downs and heartaches,
he's never left my side.
even when i hide away
where no one else can see me,
Lonely is my bestest friend
'cause Lonely never leaves me.

# POUT

9

# ADVICE 10

when i was little i was the only person who couldnt do
a cartwheel bc i was 2 scared so i tried & tried & guess
wut i still cant do a cartwheel but i gave it my best
shot & it's ok to fail as long as u try

# STICKS

you're a dimwit, a nitwit,
a halfwit and a dipshit.
a peon, a moron,
an utter bore and yawn!
imbecile! ignoramus!
vile, yucky, heinous!
a nincompoop, a ninny,
and absolutely cringey.
you're a roly-poly fatty from all the things you've eaten.
you're a jackass, an asshat, a nutcase, and a cretin.
numbskull, twerp, jack-off, pleb,
dunce, dweeb, dunderhead,
bozo, dork, buffoon, flop,
stupid, smelly, useless mop.
hold on, wait, i'm not the type
to call someone a dummy!
to whom could i ever speak this way?!
oh crap, i'm talking to me.

# BEST

everyone tells me i deserve better.
i know i deserve better.
but i don't want better.
i want you.

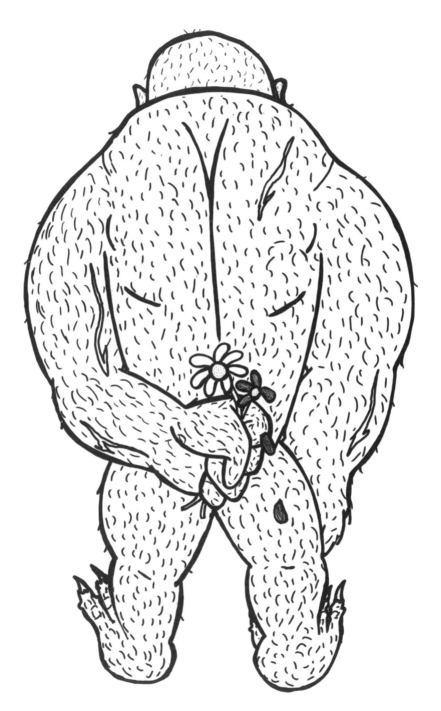

14

# HIDE

everyone's asking if i'm feeling okay.
the truth is i'm always feeling this way.
i'm just having a hard time disguising it today.

# INSPIRED

the next poem you're about to read
is because it suddenly came to me.

i hopped out of the shower soaking wet
to write it down before i could forget.
so i really hope you like it
'cause i just lost my security deposit
when i drenched my brand-new carpet
so you could read it and think "fam, this is lit!"

hope the next page was worth the compromise
of shampoo running into my eyes.

# STRANGER

he asked, can i kiss you?
she replied,
i don't know you that well.

he asked her favorite color.
come on, she said, you can do better.

so he took it to heart and better he did;
he learned about what she was like as a kid.
he listened to her friends, oh, the stories they'd tell!
he talked to her demons and learned them as well.

he became her diary the way he would hold
ever so dearly the secrets she told.
he knew all the anguish she buried inside.
he'd seen all her scars and the thoughts they implied.

but after a while he stopped asking questions
and forgot the details she'd previously mentioned.
as time went on, the distance grew
and she found a stranger in the person she knew.

so the day came, as it does so often,

that their love was laid to rest in a coffin.

as they choked on goodbye, though the bond had been
     broken,

he wanted to leave her with one parting token.


he asked, can i kiss you?

she replied,

i don't know you that well.

# HAPPY

every time
   i try to
   write a
   silly poem
it turns out
   incredibly sad.

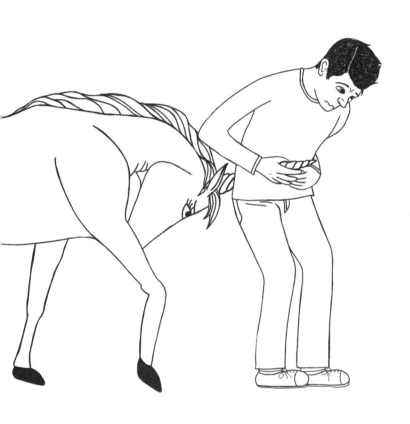

# FASHION

i've always worn my heart on my sleeve
and my feelings on my face.
you, without a doubt, could read
my mood in any case.
glad, mad, sad, or scared,
it wasn't hard to guess—
some only wear their emotions to bed,
but mine were my sunday best.
then people started critiquing my style
and criticizing my taste,
so, due to public opinion,
my revealing outfits were replaced.
they'd always been my fashion choice
but i needed to make a swap.
i've always worn my heart on my sleeve,
but now i prefer tank tops.

# RELATIVE

time
          is relative.
beauty
          is relative.
family
          is relatives.

# IRON

when i was young
my mom used to check if the iron was hot
by touching it,
and, i don't know,
i just feel like there's
a metaphor in there somewhere.

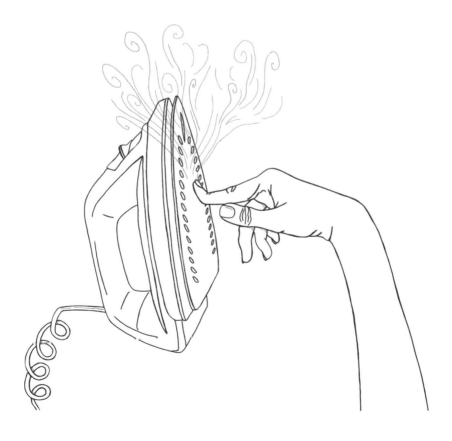

# ANXIETY

there isn't a cause that you could explain,
but i'll claw my way in like a cat in the rain.

i don't pretend to make much sense,
but i'll twist up your nerves like a barbed-wire fence.

if you find yourself without a qualm,
i'll send chills up your spine with my icy palm.

although your whole to-do list is ticked,
i'll set fire to your cheeks like a match to a wick.

no matter the time or the month or the season,
i'll ruin your day without rhyme or reason.

## STOP
you gave up
when i wanted to
    fight.
you insisted
that the future
    was gone,
you insisted
that you drive me
    home,
and the whole way
i prayed for a red light.

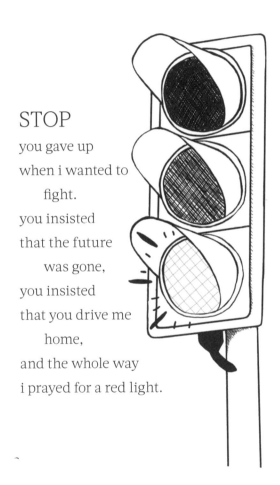

# ADVICE 4

for 25 years i told myself i couldnt do a single push-up
& now i can do 4 push-ups so dont doubt urself believe
in urself u can do anything

# LOTION

have you ever received a gift
that was placed inside of a box
that was recycled from another,
much more intriguing present?
like, you pull back the pretty paper
and you see iPad packaging,
but then you open the lid,
and inside is a lotion set?

i meet a lot of people like that.
exciting outside, disappointing inside.

don't be lotion.

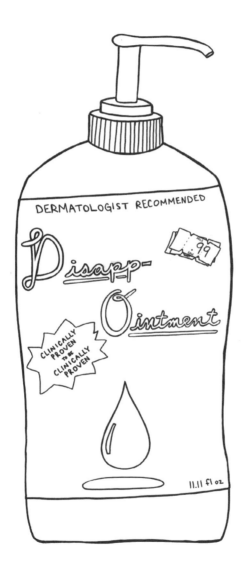

# BELT

even though i went to an inner-city public school,
we had a pretty strict dress code.
we had to wear our shirts tucked into our pants with
    a belt,
and only in about four different colors.

one day, i came to class with my new pants
that i couldn't wait to wear!
they came with a cool striped belt that matched our
    school colors.

before the bell even rang in home room, a boy pointed
and loudly said,
"YOU BOUGHT THOSE PANTS AT WALMART."
until that moment, i didn't realize that shopping at
    walmart
was something to be ashamed of.
[spoiler: it's not]
then another girl chimed in and together,
they mocked me until the bell rang.

i never wore that belt again.

a few days later, i noticed the girl who chimed in so
    urgently
was wearing the same belt. and the same pants.
i stared at them for a moment, then looked up at her face.
she quickly averted her eyes and crossed her arms
in front of her lap to hide the colored stripes.

i never said anything about it, but it perplexed me
    that she
would be so quick to chime in to make fun of that belt.

bullies are the most insecure people on the planet.

# YOU

don't worry about who you "should be";
you don't need to be ashamed.
you're perfect in the way that no one's perfect.
it's okay to not be okay.

# PHILOSOPHY

if you eat an entire pizza by yourself in the woods,
and no one's around to see it,
do the calories count?

# LOST

the truth is that i lost you;
that doesn't mean you're gone.
when i was small i lost my doll,
but retrieved it from lost and found.
one time my pet dog ran away
then found his way back home.
i once was lost in a shopping mall
and, though i felt alone,
i knew my dad would find me
just like he always did.
so "lost" just means "keep looking"
is what i learned as a kid.
"where'd you see it last"
is what my mom would always say,
so i'd retrace my steps
and i'd un-lose my stuff that way.

so, yes, i guess i lost you—
but i'll just keep on trying
to remember where i left you
so i can quit this crying.

# SMILE

the thing about a smile is it can make somebody's day.
a plain grin to a stranger can melt their cares away.
sadness, sorrow, mourning, heartbreak, hopelessness and
    grief
can all be blithely wiped away with a simple flash of teeth.
a really shitty, stupid, boring day is all worthwhile
if at the very end you were rewarded with a smile.
if you parade your row of ivories just a bit more often
the rough edges of someone's day just might begin to soften.
if more people swore to show their pretty pearly whites
i'd bet my bottom dollar you could minimize the fights.
so go ahead! wear your smirk all day and wear it proud!
wear it happy, wear it big, wear it long and loud!
stretch your mouth out to your ears until your cheeks are
    shaking!
i don't care if all that beaming means your face is breaking!
sew your lips to your gums so you never quit your simper!
i don't wanna hear a gripe, not a single
    whimper!

the thing about a frown is it can ruin
someone's day
just one glance of disapproval can
melt your joy away.
gladness, laughter, pleasure,
humor, cheerfulness and glee
can all be wistfully wiped away with a smile's absentee.
a really happy, sunny, funny day can be destroyed
if at the very end you find a grimace is employed.
if you promenade around with a healthy, hearty scowl
even the most pleasant day can start to feel quite foul.
if more people started wearing grief upon their lips
there'd be enough antipathy to sink the mightiest ships.
so don't you dare! just wipe that gloom right off your ugly
mouth!
turn the corners upwards, don't let them travel south!
SMILE, beautiful, don't be selfish! come on, don't you
know?
you're never under any fate to let your feelings show!
don't furrow your brow or scrunch your face all up in a bundle!
i don't want to hear complaints, don't let the grumbles rumble!

the thing about a smile is it's not too hard to fake it.
so i'll never let you make my day, for fear that you might
break it.

# DREAMS

my therapist tells me what my dreams mean
& i believe him
the way you believe your teacher
when he tells you
what a poem means.

# FLUENT

as of late, since this book deal, i speak in strictly poetry.
my sentences are metered and heroic couplets flow
    freely.
every minuscule moment is a latent free-form verse;
my hyperbole or imagery, i'm not sure which is worse.
every brute or object is a potential metaphor;
my art form is heartache peppered with delusions of
    grandeur.
silly similes slip off my tongue to an insufferable degree.
each turn i take to talk is an ostentatious soliloquy.
dousing my friends in leaden pretension is something
    i do fear;
i wish that i could take a break, but my deadline's
    growing near.

# CONCEALER

i wear makeup because i have acne.
i have acne because i wear makeup.

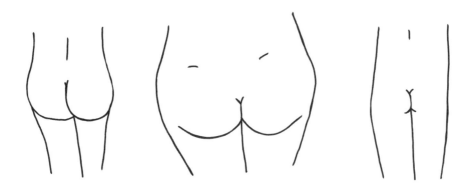

## ADVICE 1

when i was younger girls asked "does this make my butt look big" in like a concerned way & now girls ask "does my butt look big" in an excited way so dont worry ur butt will be trendy some day

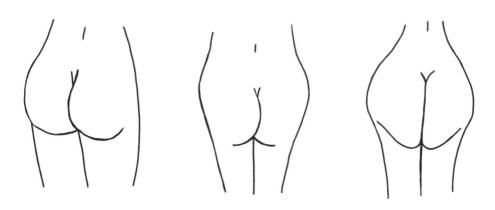

## STUNTED

why is it that

i cry when i'm angry,
and fight when i'm sad?
i laugh when i'm uneasy,
and stifle giggles when i'm glad?
i'm silent when i'm scared,
but speak when i'm unsure?
i'm emotionally impaired
and viscerally immature.

# METAPHOR

am i crazy, [*rhetorical question*]
or does it seem that
you can use your phone as a coaster,
toss it around like a hacky sack,
punt it across the street to your buddy
who then takes it to the train station and lays it on the
    tracks
for a high-five with the next oncoming locomotive,
play a game of tennis with it in place of a ball,
send it through a washing machine with bricks,
dance on it in high heels in a puddle of liquor–
and it's fine.

but the second you drop it half a foot
from your plush bed to your carpeted floor
atop your cashmere rug,

       i t   s h a t t e r s.

this is a very millennial metaphor
for the human psyche.

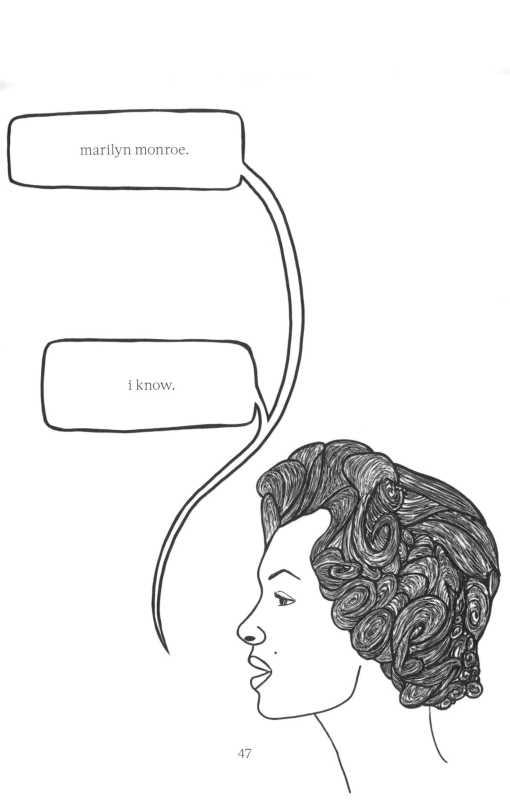

# CHEATER

i accidentally used your toothbrush today,
but i didn't mind,
'cause it's the closest i can get to your kiss.

then i remembered where
your mouth has been,
and i got really fucking pissed.

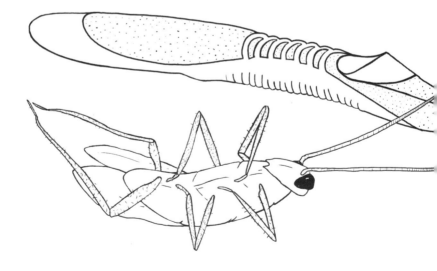

## TIME

isn't is funny
how you can go your entire life
without someone

then one day
you can't imagine a minute
without them

# BIRD

i jumped today and i survived.
everyone assumed that i wanted to die;
i just wanted to know what it's like to fly.

# CHIVALRY

i'm not some no-brained bimbo
and i'm not some helpless girl.
i am fucking remarkable
and i deserve the world.
i don't need you to open my door,
but the gesture would be nice.
i don't need you to buy my meal;
the offer would suffice.
i don't need to be taken care of,
but it'd be cool to know you care.
i'm a holographic charizard:
highly desired and rare.
yo,
i even drop pokémon references
'cause i'm fuckin' dope as shit.
i'm good with just me, i don't need you
not even a tiny bit.

but need and want are different
and i can't deny the latter.
when it comes to you, autonomy
just really doesn't matter.
but i don't ask for all your time
or my weight in gold.
all i want is a good-morning text
and a fucking hand to hold.
of all the things i listed,
just know this to be true:
i want you in my life, my love,
as much as i don't need you.

# ADVICE 5

beware of the power of persuasion one time i
convinced an entire table of ppl that a piece of
chocolate pie tasted like mac & cheese like they all
agreed it was nuts anyway dont believe everything u
hear be ur own person think 4 urself

## VOMIT

how is it:

you can throw up from a food you love
and all of a sudden hate it
regardless of all the other times
you enjoyed yourself when you ate it,

but for some reason:

hearts don't work like gag reflexes;
when it comes to people we care for,
we'll just keep right on indulging and
let them make us sick over and over.

# PETS

a cute little dog! a cute little puppy!
mommy will get me one if i'm lucky!
i'll walk him and love him and watch him grow!
he'll fetch and bring back the ball that i throw!

      a cute little fishy! a cute little fish
      in a cute little bowl with bright rocks is my wish!
      i'll sprinkle a bit of his little fish feed
      and he'll gobble it up with his guppy-mouth
         greed!

a cute little kitty! a cute little cat!
he'll arch up his back and chase a fat rat!
he'll be moody and lazy and take a sun bath,
i'll give him some catnip when i need a laugh!

      i love all my pets! i love them so dearly!
      they're my best friends, truly, sincerely!
      i'll keep getting pets even though i cry
      every time my cute little bestie dies!

# CONTINUED

pets are weird. people getting pets are weird.

think about it.

we choose these creatures to love and care for.

they become our best friends, our children,

the furry shoulder to cry on when no one else is around.

     you depend on one another and you fill their
       bowl.

     they need to eat, we need to feed our soul.

we teach them tricks and make them do "people things."

we post photos online and include them on our
    christmas cards.

     we can't believe we could love a thing so much,
     and they become an unwavering emotional
      crutch.

we build an uncomplicated, pure, everlasting love,

and we do this all knowing damn well

that this precious little beast will, more likely than not,

die long before us.

we become so connected to this . . . being

with full knowledge that someday,

we will lose them.

we will miss them.

we will hurt.

we will suffer.

but we knew this.

we knew this before we went to Petco in the first place.

but still we went.

and still we loved.

and still they died.

and still we hurt.

# CUT

her hand trembled around the sharp, cold metal
as she looked at her distorted face in the mirror:

"just do it,"
she told her reflection.

    "don't do it,"
    her reflection replied.

"come on, pussy!"
she shouted at the glass.

    "you're going to regret this,
    you always do,"
    the glass warned back.

"no one gives a shit if i do it,"
she reminded them both.

    "this is a permanent decision
    based on a temporary emotion,"
    the mirror pleaded.

"hair grows back, dumbass."

    *snip*

# FAIR

life isn't fair
but it's unfair to everyone
so that's fair i guess.

# ORGANS

a man told me that in the hour before he proposed to
    his wife,
she kept complaining that she had to pee.
they couldn't find a restroom,
so, he popped the question anyway.
she said yes.
she didn't realize until hours later,
after they had dinner and called everyone
in their contacts to share the news,
that she never did pee.

may your heart always be fuller than your bladder.

# QUOTES

"i'm not gonna lie."
*—someone who's about to lie*


"i hate drama."
*—a very dramatic person*


"i don't care what people think."
*—an insecure individual*


"i'm not like other girls."
*—a particularly predictable girl*


"i would like a snack."
*—me*

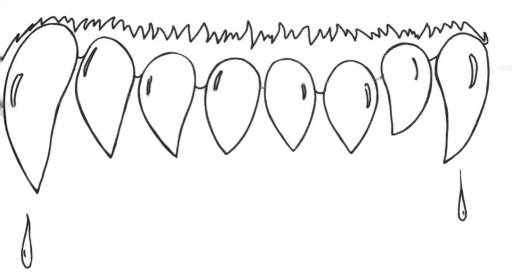

## DOG

i'm a wounded animal;
if you corner me, i'll bite.
but, baby, i don't want to hurt you;
i bare my teeth in fright.

# RESOLUTION

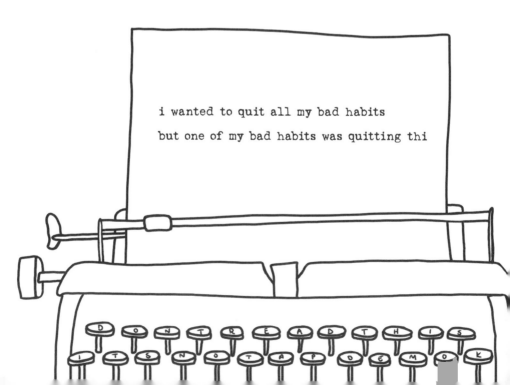

i wanted to quit all my bad habits

but one of my bad habits was quitting thi

# MATCH

sometimes you need to pick yourself up,
brush yourself off,
take a good, hard look in the mirror
and ask yourself,
"would i swipe right?"

# DOLLHOUSE

a paper airplane soaring by
plaster clouds in a concrete sky
a tinkering toy box lullaby–
what a pleasant place to live!

matchstick buildings line cardboard roads
a blue paint pond filled with loads
of clay fish and silicone toads–
what a charming place to live!

trees and shrubs propped up with velcro
where all the porcelain boys and girls go
lightbulbs glare on a saran wrap window–
what a lovely place to live!

a magnificent mountain drawn in pencil
people mass-produced by stencil
they warn against it, but you went still–
what a boring place to live!

silk petals on plastic stems
silk hair on plastic friends
silk stains and plastic bends–
what a lonely place to live!

mouths are glued and lips are sewn
hands are tied and punches are thrown
permanent marker lines are drawn–
what a hostile place to live!

families held together by string
cross-stitched lives rip at the seam
close the curtain but start the scene–
what a fucked-up place to live!

mommy cries at the ceramic sink
daddy fixes a grown-up drink
isn't it strange and funny to think–
this is how we choose to live?

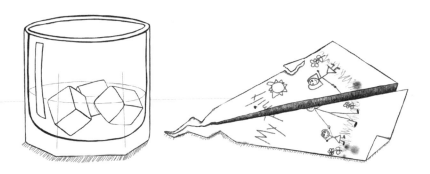

# DEVIATED

these nights are awfully boring
without your awful snoring.

## SHH

good things happen when my mind is silent;
thinking has never done me any good.

# HOME

sally filed for divorce
much to tommy's horror.
she abandoned their apartment
but still lived in every corner.
as he looked at his surroundings
our boy tom took inventory–
each knick-knack and nook and cranny
told a different story.
so tommy decided frantically
he couldn't bear the sheets
that he shared with his dear sally
so he sleeps out on the streets.
it's not quite the perfect life
that tommy had envisioned;
in place of his ex-wife he finds
his solace with the pigeons.
he keeps all his belongings
in a stolen shopping cart
and the nightly chill of pavement
soothes his aching, broken heart.
he's often hungry, often scared,
but what else can he do?
it's better to be homeless
than have no one to come home to.

# POETRY

i want to write you into a poem but can't find the right
  synonym.
every time i try it's just revision after revision!
i can't construct a simile without the right comparison
so i'm sure you understand the predicament i'm working in.
i wouldn't have an issue if my hunt was for an antonym:
repulsive, boring, lame, stupid, irksome imperfection.
but there is no single word in any language ever written
to describe the impossible attributes that you, my dear, were
  given.

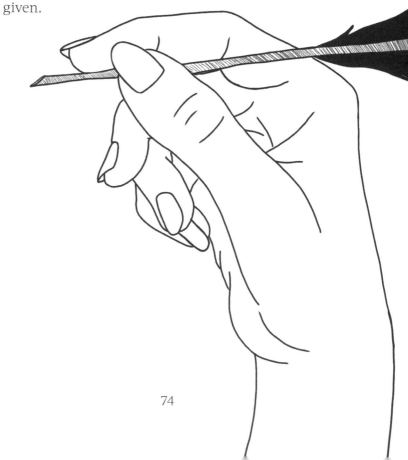

# FLIES

they told me, "you'd catch more flies with honey."
but i don't want to catch flies.

i want to kill them.

# TEASE

if a guy doesn't answer your texts for three years
does that mean he's not interested
or is he just playing hard to get?
whatever, i don't mind taking it slow.

# ARMS

your embrace was once my safety blanket,
swaddled so tight and snug.
encompassed in security,
i could die inside your hug.

your embrace is now a straitjacket,
so tight that i can't move.
it's holding me together but
i'll die in a padded room.

CHECK

1. Sometimes i keep old to-do ✓
2. lists around when i'm feeling ✓
3. down on myself to feel like ✓
4. i've accomplished a lot. ✓

5. turns out none of them ✓
6.
7. are completed.

8.
9. wow i feel like shit.

10.

# ADVICE 3

always lock the bathroom door bc 10/10 times it
prevents an awkward situation but do it even if ur
home alone bc if a murderer comes u'll want to have
time to pull up ur leggings & die with dignity

# DOLLY

i'll be your little rag doll when you're feeling kinda bored,
even if it means that when you're not i'll be ignored.
i'll ask to be a real girl though you treat me like i'm fake
and toss me like a ball without concern that i might
    break.
if you'd rather play with trucks or build things with
    your blocks,
just shut the lid and turn the key to lock me in your
    toy box.
i'll still be here waiting when you say you wanna play,
and every day i'll sit and pray you don't throw me away.
'til that comes, i'll wait for you to choose me as your
    plaything
'cause every single time you want to use me it's amazing.
i'll admit that when you put me back my spirit falls–
i don't know whoever said that boys don't play with dolls.

# GONE

i don't fear death.
i fear the end of all my thoughts and dreams
that will disappear into nothingness when i die.

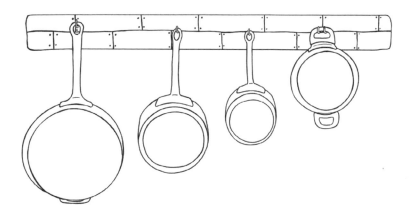

## OCD

i'm not the best at organizing thoughts,
but no one's better at organizing pots.

i'm ineffective at handling stress,
but i'm an expert at handling mess.

life is kinda tough to handle,
but it's a breeze to dust a mantel.

the fear of losing control is mighty,
but at least your closet's neat and tidy.

# LOOPHOLE

you have three wishes—

you can't wish for more wishes,
you can't wish for love,
you can't wish to bring anyone back
    from the dead.

first wish, i wish that those rules didn't apply to me—

second, i wish for unlimited wishes.

third, i wish for channing tatum,

fourth, i wish for mouse, my cat, to come back to life.

fifth, i want a double cheeseburger with no onions.

sixth,

damn it.

86

# SAD

isfied

## GIFT

i know it hurt your feelings when i returned what you
    called presents.
i wish that i could keep them, but they remind me of
    your presence.

# FATE

if opposites attract, my soul mate is going to be
funny, easygoing, charming, attractive, exciting,
adventurous, affectionate, amiable, courageous,
intelligent, rational, affable, brave, humble, neat,
well-tempered, patient, polite, confident, sensible,
emotionally stable, and just an all-around gem.

lucky me!

# PLEASE

i know, babe.
but i wish you'd drop dead, babe.

91

# IRONY

ninety-eight percent of your body is made up of $H_2O$.

ninety. eight. percent.

stay hydrated, or else you'll die of thirst.

but did you know you can also die from drinking too
    much water?

it's called water intoxication.

google it, bitch.

this thing that you literally need to keep you alive will
    literally kill you.

ninety-eight percent of you will turn on you in a second.


water is the reason i have trust issues.

# ANSWER

we ask ourselves, from womb to grave,
what are the secrets to life?
have we created love to save
ourselves from unwavering strife?
why bear the pain of childbirth
just to fade and wither away?
why were we put on this earth
if we aren't allowed to stay?
why do we read books and learn
just to forget when we are dead?
why is it we so anxiously squirm
and await that day with dread?
furthermore, who put us here?
but more importantly, why?
"i'll live forever!" is insincere,
but alas, we'll always try.
some will seek the fountain of youth
to reverse the signs of age.
some will search for unholy truth
with séances and sage.
others want the holy grail
or, maybe, just the quest.
but all of them will surely fail
and expire like the rest.

that is all a myth, of course—
just stories! it's all a lie!
the secret to life (from a reliable source)[1]
is simply, *just don't die.*

---

1.     wikipedia

# ADVICE 7

deal with ur problems right away dont ignore them
it's like when u drop an ice cube & it seems like no big
deal so u ignore it then it turns into a puddle & before
u know it ur sock is wet & that all could have been
avoided so dont run from ur problems or else u'll end
up with wet socks

# NEW

heartbroken women
cut their hair
in hopes that
removing dead ends
will somehow
make them feel
alive

*again*

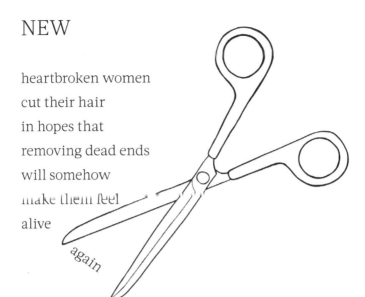

# LA

you're gonna miss me every time it rains
in this town that floods from lack of drains.
the storms here are light and very rare
so the city streets are unprepared.
but you and me, we like the water
and the eerie chill that comes thereafter.
so when i'm gone and you're stuck in traffic
and all the drivers start to panic
'cause they're paralyzed by soggy weather,
you'll feel my absence more than ever.

with every drip of every drop,
you'll think of me and your heart will stop.
even if only thrice a year,
you'll hear me purring in your ear.
like the momentary strike of lightning
you'll close your eyes and see me dancing.
i'll be the ghost you don't believe in.
i'll drench your mind in ways not even
your windshield wipers can sweep clean.
every time it rains, you'll remember me.

# ADULTOLESCENCE

have you ever met a kid who wasn't a kid?
who did all the things mommies and daddies did?
who didn't have friends or play games much,
but cooked and cleaned and cared for babies and such?

give that kid a hug.

# PRISONER

you asked a question; i have an answer.
i'd speak but liquid nitrogen
has spread through my body like cancer.

the room feels smaller as it fills with the quiet.
in my head is a crowded room,
but you can't hear the riot.

there's a tinier me trapped inside of me.
she's locked up in my [rib]cage
and i threw away the key.

she's loud as hell but she's having little luck,
'cause every time she tries to talk
i tell that bitch to shut up.

you want me to talk but i'm sitting silent.
it seems like i have nothing to say
but the screaming inside is violent.

# YUM

if the world ended tomorrow, what would you do today?
i'd hurriedly make my way
to an all-you-can-eat buffet.

# ENTERTAINER

all i've ever wanted is to make people happy.

and to get rich doing it.

and also fame.

but only because that means i could make more
people happy.

who would give me more money

# BULLY

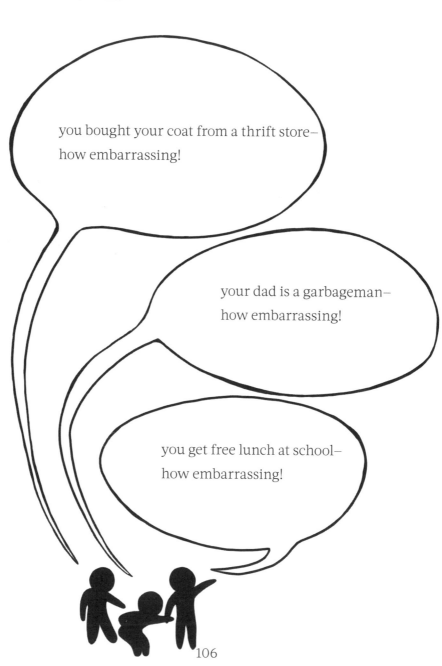

you actually believe that this shit matters—
how embarrassing!

# STATS

here are some facts about love!

2% of marriages are high school sweethearts :ʼ)
20% of couples meet online \ (•o•) \
and 17% of them get married <3
70% of married people cheat (º﹏º)
and 50% of marriages end in divorce <|3
but none of this matters because
100% of relationships end in death! :D

# ABUSE

i'm so sorry
you were in
the blast radius
when some
delicate flower
had his ego
shattered.

K

# ADVICE 11

ive always been afraid to put eyeshadow under my eye
bc i thought my eyes looked too droopy but one day i
started doing it & someone commented on my insta
pic "this is ur best look yet!" & i realized wow i should
have been doing this for years but then someone else
commented "ur makeup looks like shit" & i realized
wow you cant make everyone happy so just make u
happy

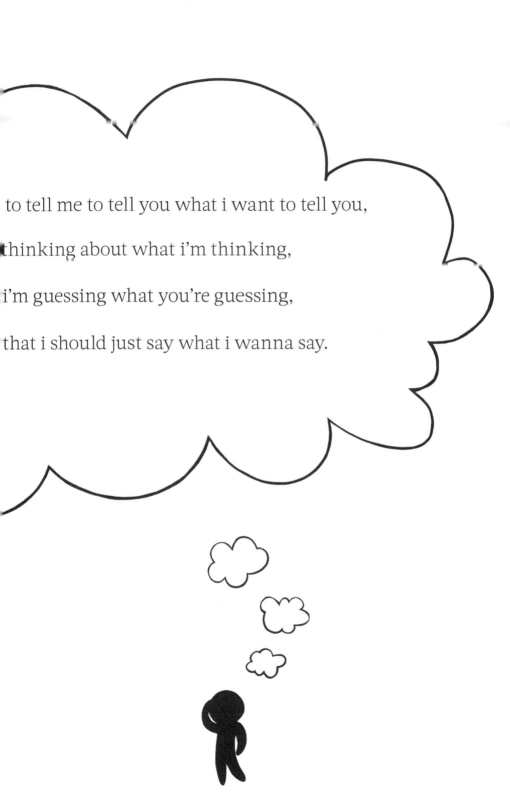

# WORRY

i tried to take a nap today. everything was great.

it was dark, but not so dark that my body thought it
was bedtime.

it was warm, but not so warm that i had to poke my
feet out.

it was so unbelievably comfortable, i could lie there
forever.

but then, i remembered the alarm clock that i set.

i knew i could only rest for thirty minutes,

and in about twenty-four, that repulsive honking
would start.

napping is the best. waking up from a nap is the worst.

i became fixated on the idea of this cozy dreamland
coming to an end.

instead of feeling the cloud-like pillow under my head,

i felt the dread of the alarm inside my mind.

instead of enjoying the blanket nestled over my body,

i suffered the expectation of imminent screeching
looming over my thoughts.

i spent so much time anticipating having to wake up
that i never fell asleep.

## HYPOCRITE

ever notice that the word "synonym"
doesn't have a synonym?

# ADVICE 15

never let someone else be the reason u wake up in the
morning

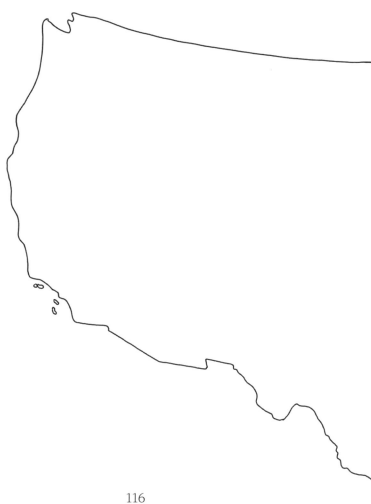

# GEOGRAPHY

my heart is in pittsburgh
my brain is in california
my fingers are in your hair
so let's cut the small talk

# WASTED

i'm way more fun drunk.
not in like a,
      "i'm really fun when i'm drunk"
kinda way, but more in like a,
      "you need to be drunk in order to have fun
         around me"
kinda way.

# EW

you're disgusting

ly perfect

# CATHOLIC

i gave up for lent.

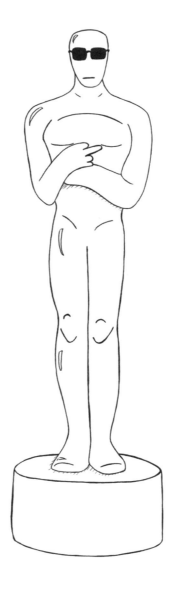

# DESERVED

i wish the oscars had a "best extra" category.
i would love to see jessica lowry take home the award
for her outstanding performance as "girl in lobby #3."
her ability to fill space and pantomime conversation is
unprecedented and she should be celebrated.

# LIVE

things won't get better if you're gone.
you can't feel relief if you're a carcass.
if it's the shadows that you're running from,
remember that dead eyes only see darkness.

# ADVICE 9

when i was a kid i thought id never be able to swallow
a pill & now i can swallow two pills at a time so ur
capable of more than u could even imagine in ur
wildest dreams

# GHOST

listening for answers that would never be heard,
i realized that silence speaks louder than words.
seeking explanation, i felt blind and deaf.
i don't care that you're gone, i just hate how you left.

# HURRY

good things happen to those who wait.
except when there's free food involved.
that shit goes quick.

## BURN

i smashed my smoke detector
because i'd rather die a fiery painful death
than listen to it judge me
every time i cook bacon.

126

## 20/20

he told me i should trust him—
i had no reason not to.
he filled me up, right to the brim,
and my feelings quickly grew.

he said he'd never hurt me
and to this day he had not.
he said he'd never hurt me,
but it seemed he soon forgot.

i turned the other cheek when
he would talk to other girls.
they were a vacation,
but to him, i was the world.

he promised he'd protect me,
then he struck me limb to limb.
guess i never knew he meant
i needed protection from him.

he pleaded for forgiveness
as i fell down to the ground.
he said he had a sickness
and he needed me around.

again, he had to grovel
when my face hit the cement.
i crumbled like the gravel
when he offered his lament.

he said i was his future,
and so i took his word.
he said i was his future,
then the rest was all a blur.

they told me to leave sooner.
i couldn't do that, never!
blood and bruises disappear
but true love is for forever!

he said he'd never leave me;
on his mother's grave, he swore.
so i guess it kinda shook me
when he walked right out the door.

they told me to get away;
there was no reason i could find.
i guess i learned the hard way!
lesson being,
        love is blind(ing pain).

# PUNISHMENT

if you plan on giving someone the silent treatment,
make sure they give a fuck about what you have to say

# HERO

like lots of elderly people, my great-grandma was hard
    of hearing.
like lots of hard of hearing people, my great-grandma
    wore a hearing aid.
my family is loud, and we are annoying, and there are
    a lot ol' us.
sometimes at holidays or obligatory bonding time,
after all the kids had too much sugar or all the adults
    had too much liquor,
my great-grandma would simply turn down her
    hearing aid.
just like that, she switched the room to mute.
at the turn of a knob, she turned our bickering into a
    silent movie.
she was able to hush the world and
    create her own peace.

her disability was her superpower.

## LOVEBOAT

next time you pour everything you have into someone,
make sure they don't have any leaks.

## PRANKSTER

God has a sick sense of humor.
He put men and women on this earth,
then told them to not only coexist, but to reproduce.
he built their bodies to survive on one another,
yet built their brains to agree on virtually nothing.


aaaahhhhhh you got us so good!

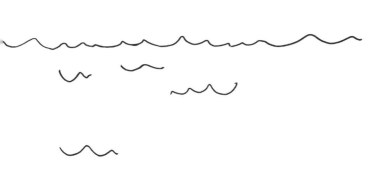

# CRAVINGS

cheese cravings are a sign you have a calcium deficiency.
it also signifies that you really like cheese.

if you're craving red meat, you may have an iron
    deficiency.
also, hamburgers are delicious.

a desire for salty food means you need more essential
    fatty acids.
alternatively, that you like nonessential fatty food.

if you eat chocolate in copious amounts, you're
    lacking magnesium.
that, and self-control.

# NAP

you woke a part of me i thought was dead,
but i guess it was just sleeping.

# EARLYBIRD

i awake before the sun with a head as clear as ice.
the thought of having zero thoughts i thought would
  be quite nice.
but i taste the cold and feel the dark the moment i
  wake up.
it's like my body misses you before my mind can
  catch up.

# MOTHERGOOSE

one two, buckle my shoe
three four, better lock the door
five six, why the fuck are you
taking demands from a nursery rhyme
grow a backbone if you can't even
stand up to a poem written for
preschoolers you stand no chance
in the real world start thinking
for yourself damn

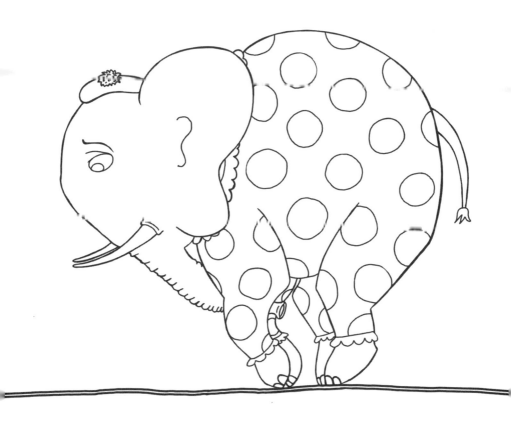

## LOVE

i saw a very old man buying pads for a woman today.

that's the kind of love i want.

old man buying feminine hygiene products kind of love.

# WEB

the dislike button is my biggest critic.
am i a good person? check my analytics.
i'm lucky, i know, i don't mean to misinform—
i just *need* a moment i don't *need* to perform.
i realize i'm blessed, but if i may spin it:
when you're you for a living, you can't take a minute
to process your thoughts of confusion or sorrow.
we are yesterday's stars of tomorrow,
   and we are tomorrow's yesterday's news.

"what's next?" is the question i can't escape from.
i'm not yet the person i'm meant to become.
i want to do more, much more! in fact,
i want to dance and sing and act!
but i can't get hired 'til i promise to tweet it
so i'll just film, edit, post, and repeat it.
i'll stick to schedule 'cause my biggest fear
is to get lost in the crowd and disappear,
   but, some days, that doesn't seem so bad.

the pursuit of happiness sounds obscene
when your source of joy is numbers on a screen.
so you tell me, what's my worth today?
do you love me as much as yesterday?
quantify me, give me my rating!
i hope you can forgive my click-baiting
but the conundrum is this life that's conditioned
me to treat every day as if it's an audition
            for a part i'm not even sure that i want.

we're fragile and scared and nobody cares
'cause we're the millennial millionaires.
fuck your skills or the things you did,
you take selfies for a living, your opinion's invalid.
compromise yourself to gain a fan.
monetize your life any way you can.
i'll tell you whatever you need me to say
just to stay relevant another day,
            so please, like, comment, and subscribe.

# ADVICE 8

be grateful for everyone u meet bc every ex every
shitty friend was in ur life for a reason even if it was
just to introduce u to a cool movie or make u listen to
ur favorite new band 4 the first time & if not honestly
they seem kinda boring af anyway so good riddance

## QUESTION

are you happy,

      or are you not sad?

# RECYCLE

i don't know what it is that i see in you,
and i don't even know what i want.
i don't understand what you came here for.
can't you find some other heart to haunt?

i think it was always meant to end this way;
there never was a time we were in sync.
i can't pretend to reminisce, there were no "good
    ol' days,"
but please don't try to tell me what to think.

i don't know what it is that i think should be.
if i could, i don't know what it is i'd change.
i have these expectations that aren't fair of me.
maybe i just really like the pain.

i don't know why it is that i can't talk to you;
i've always worn my feelings on my shirt.
it doesn't make much sense that we would want
    this still;
but i think secretly, deep down, we like to hurt.

the game was always how can i manipulate
this lust to make it seem like something real?
i know you think that everything we had was fake,
but i won't try to tell you how to feel.

i can't begin to say what you mean to me.
i can't even begin to even tell you why.
as much as i would never like to see you again,
please don't make this poem our last goodbye.

# SISTERS

i have to go make a bottle
and feed the baby.

# THERAPY

how do i feel?

the entire car ride here
i kept envisioning
a gruesome head-on collision
with a fucking semi
and i unbuckled my seatbelt
just in case.

that's how i feel.

## SUP

you really hurt my feelings
but you're the person i talk to when my feelings are hurt
so this is kinda awkward.

anyway what's up?

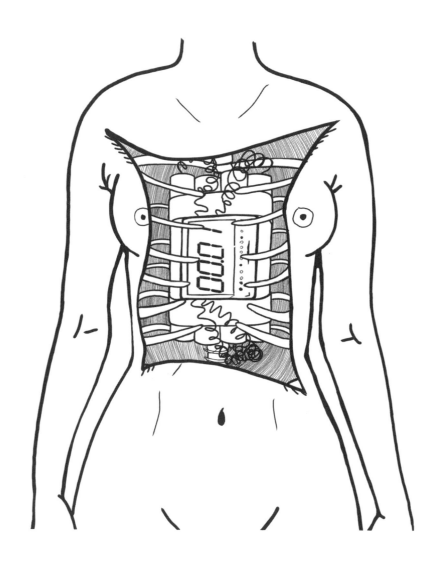

# BOOM

could you, sir, if you don't mind,
defuse the bomb in my chest?
if it's not too much trouble, could you be so kind
as to solve this wiry mess?
i know what the diminishing number means,
i'm running out of seconds it seems,
i'm about to be blown to smithereens,
and the ticking is making me anxious.

so please, sir, if you can spare the time,
defuse the bomb in my chest?

# HMM

i wonder what dying feels like.
you, too?
i'll let you know when i find out.
oh, wait.

## HOST

God is a gracious host
but he isn't too polite to let you know
when you've overstayed your welcome
and it's time to leave the party.

# CATFISH

he wanted to be ten years younger.
she wanted to be twenty pounds lighter.
so they played pretend,
then they finally met,
turns out they were perf for each other!

# SAFE

"be careful!" they warn.
"be cautious!" they say.
"if you keep living like this,
you'll die one day!"

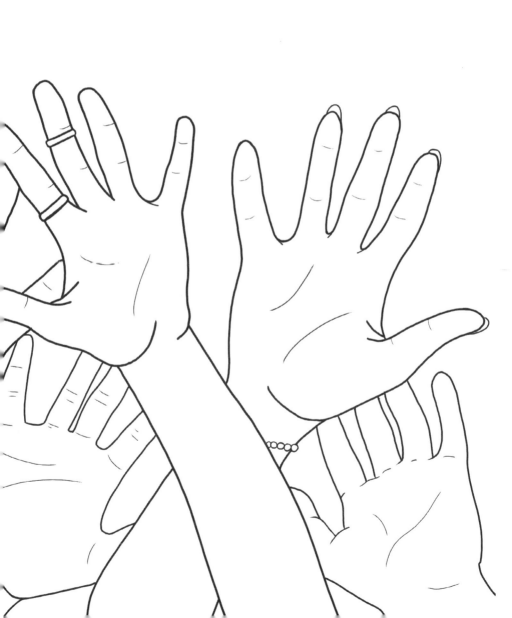

# SUN

i never gave a damn about a sunset.
i never cared to look up at the sky.
watched my sister's birth & my brother's death
& never stopped to ask Him "why?"
i never tried to find the gold
at the rainbow's end,
& i never once a secret told
to a childhood friend.
i never tried to count the stars
in orion's belt.
when the earth & moon aligned with mars
not a feeling was felt.
i really couldn't give a shit
about a solar eclipse,
& i really can't be bothered
with marigolds or tulips.
i never really notice
the beauty of the trees,
the butterflies, the dragonflies,
the ladybugs & bees.
i haven't looked for shapes in clouds
since i was a youngling,
& i don't give a damn

if i never hear a blue jay sing.
mountains aren't majestic
if you don't pay them any mind.
my vision is fine. perfect, really.
but i might as well be blind.

all this looking down
will surely be my demise,
but i'd rather die than wake up in time
to watch a fucking sunrise.

# LIKE

like, i didn't think i was like, gonna like it the way
that i like it but, like, i like it.

# LIGHTBULBS

i stopped loving my lover-
that light burnt out.
i stopped calling my mother-
i smashed that bulb to bits.
i'm wary of my friends-
now there's glass strewn about.
i stopped loving myself,
and now i'm left in darkness

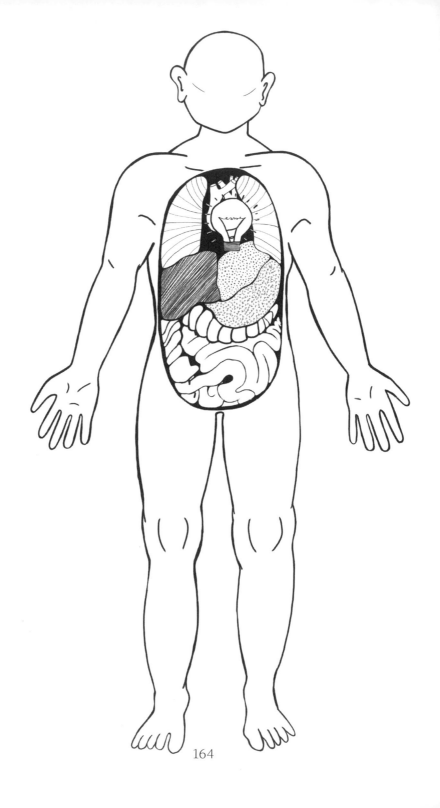

164

# ANATOMY

take a moment and close your eyes.
when you imagine your insides, what do you see?
do you see pink tunnels and white bones and a juicy,
    red heart?
do you imagine blue veins and green spleens
like some textbook coloring book
or some magic school bus amusement park ride?
i hate to be the bearer of bad news,
but under your layers of ivory, peachy, black, brown,
    or yellow skin
is total darkness.
there is no light inside of you.
the color of you is the color of the back of your eyelids
when i ask you to close your eyes and imagine your
    insides.
your heart, for all the long years of your life,
has been beating in the dark.

# ERASER

i need you to un-say some stuff you said
and un-do the things you did
so perhaps, possibly one day
i can maybe un-love you, kid.

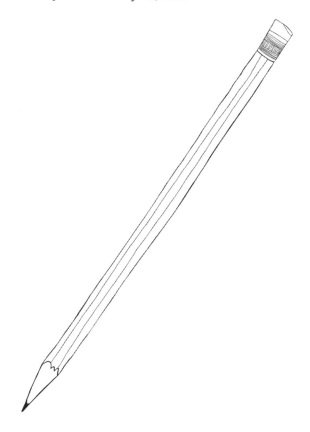

# ADVICE 2

when im sober mcdonalds seems like the worst
possible decision but when im drunk it seems like the
best possible choice so if something in ur life doesnt
seem right maybe just try looking at it through a
different lens & also mix vodka with grapefruit juice
it's surprisingly refreshing

# Link

in bio

## COFFEE

i woke up and put on a pot of coffee.

i am my father.

i left the pot on and burnt it.

i am my mother.

# NAIL POLISH

ever notice that manicurists never have their nails done?
ladies and gentlemen, the american dream.

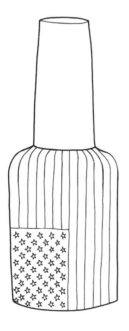

# HEIRLOOM

he snatched an innocent, porcelain angel from the
  shelf and smashed it against the wall.
delicate shrapnel filled the air and searched for a place
  to settle.

"that was my great-great-grandmother's," she sobbed.

she sent a crystal vase plummeting towards the dusty,
  scuffed floor.
tiny, lethal diamonds scattered, waiting to lodge
  themselves into an unsuspecting heel.

"that was my great-great-grandson's," he scoffed.

# SNAP

this thing we're doing,
it's merely a photocopy of what we had.
just some flat thought of a beautiful moment passed.
but i'll take it for now.
i'll pin it above my headboard and look at it before i go
      to sleep
every single night for however long it takes
until it blends in with the walls and i forget it's there.
then, one day, maybe it'll catch my eye again
and i'll look at it with fondness and affection.
maybe i'll feel a whisper of the warmth you brought,
or maybe i'll feel a hint of exhaustion.
but memories will always just be that.
so i'll toss it in the pile with the rest
or add it to my photo album that i keep in the attic.
the past is for visiting, not living.

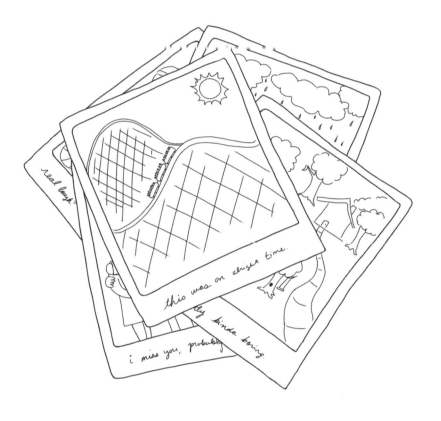

# FRIGHTENED

i'm trembling,
but not in fear.
you terrify me,
but i'm not scared.

# RICH

there once was a boy named sonny
he never had much money
so he busted his ass
now he flies first class
and life is sweet as honey

sonny slaves away
he has no time to play
he swallows a pontoon
of pills by noon
just to get through the day

# CHANGE

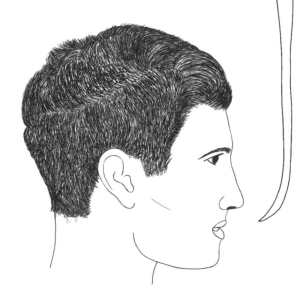

lately, i just don't feel like myself.

## ADVICE 17

it's pretty shocking that racism still exists it's literally a matter of black & white like say u like kittens ur going to like kittens whether its a black kitten or a white kitten the color of the kitten doesnt change the fact that it's a kitten so can we all just chill with judging by color because fur is just fur & kittens are great oh & if ur a dog person feel free to replace the word kitten with puppy

# EMOTIONS

if you can't decide whether to laugh or cry
just laugh until you cry.

# SANTA

there's always that asshole in every class who tells the
   others,

>    "Santa's not real!
>    you think that chump flies across the world
>    in his reindeer-powered automobile?
>    and carries all those presents
>    on his tiny little sleigh?
>    he'd never pull it off, it's impossible!
>    come on, gimme a break!"

it's like, when they lost the magic themselves,
they wanted to steal it from everyone else.

but if they find out they're wrong they're gonna be
      pissed;
what if santa's real, you're just on the naughty list?

# CERTAIN

i think i guess i know
that you probably definitely
maybe for sure are
potentially the one for me.

# SELF-HELP

they say focus on me, be the best i can be.
i think i've had enough time to myself;
i'm ready to share it with someone else.
if i'm honest, i've had enough of me.

# CLEAN

i've got a head full of nightmares,
a heart full of rage,
a belly full of liquor,
and a sink full of dishes.

i'll start with the dishes.

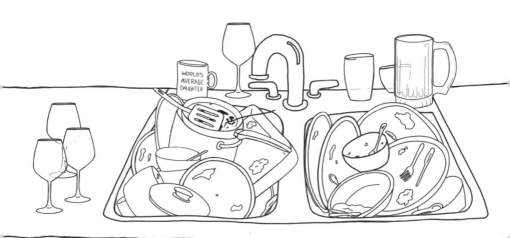

# BREAKFAST

did you ever wake up in the morning
and really want a bowl of cereal
but you were out of milk
so instead of milk you used orange juice
and instead of cereal you used vodka?

# ALIENS

people are always looking for evidence that aliens exist,
but the proof is right in front of us!

you know that gymnast that holds that other gymnast
above her head with one hand while doing a triple
    pirouette
while that other gymnast touches her foot to the back
    of her head
then dismounts by spiraling upwards forty times?
        alien.
you know that eight-year-old singer that auditions on
    some competition show
and causes the hair of every single man woman and
    child in the audience
and everyone viewing at home from the comfort of
    their couches
to stand straight up on the backs of their necks?
        alien.
you know that regular-looking guy
that shoots a basketball backwards across the entire
    court,
blindfolded, and in one effortless try
you hear a perfect, untainted "swish"?
        alien.

you know that person who created that
    robot girlfriend
that moves its face all human-like and
    learns your interests
and has conversations with you about cars
    or cooking or hentai
or whatever it is that you like to do in your
    alone time?
        alien.

they're here! they're awesome!
they're winning championships and
    making cool apps and starring in
    viral videos!
just let the aliens live already!

# ADVICE 16

im not superstitious but if u see a lucky penny pick it up if u spill some salt throw it over ur shoulder if u see a falling star make a wish if u can avoid it then dont step on a crack cuz honestly it prob wont help but it sure as hell wont hurt & also i dont see any reason u have to walk under a ladder

# WISH

if i had one wish, it would be to never have a typo in a
    poem agian

# FLYING

if you're afraid to fly,
just remember:

you're more likely to die on the way to the airport
than in an actual plane crash.

oh, that didn't make you less nervous to fly?
it just made you more nervous to drive?

my bad.

# RUN

in middle school i always wanted to join a sport or team,
but between the sign-up fee, the price of uniforms . . .
it just wasn't in the cards.
one day, i found out that track & field was only $25 to
    join!
i had saved my christmas money and i signed up
immediately.

i couldn't wait to run!

the first practice, i was so excited to feel like i
was finally a part of something
and had somewhere to go after school.
the first practice, someone made fun of my
shoes because they were from PayLess.

i ran!

that's one of my most painful memories.
not because some preteen twat said something cruel
to me,
but because i let it affect my decision
and deter me from doing something that i wanted to do.

from that day on, i swore to myself that i would never allow others' negativity to prevent me from being happy.

from that day on, i promised myself i would never

run.

# PHONE

phones keep getting slimmer,
and people keep buying them.
cases keep getting thicker,
and people keep buying them.

my phone feels the same,
but my wallet feels slimmer.

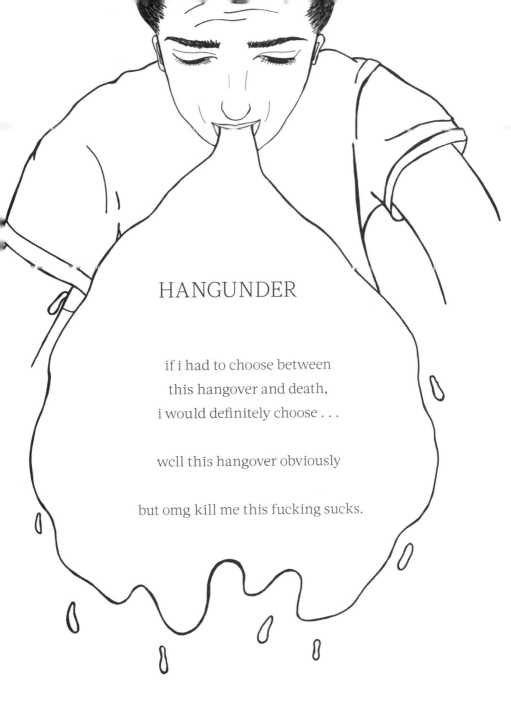

# HANGUNDER

if i had to choose between
this hangover and death,
i would definitely choose . . .

well this hangover obviously

but omg kill me this fucking sucks.

# DEPRESSION

when life is great and nothing's wrong,
i'll stay in your mind like a catchy song.

when you come up for air and you're feeling free,
i'll weigh you down like lead boots in the sea.

if you try to wash me down the drain,
thicker than mud, i'll stick to your brain.

when you're filled with joy without concern,
i'll hollow you out like a jack-o'-lantern.

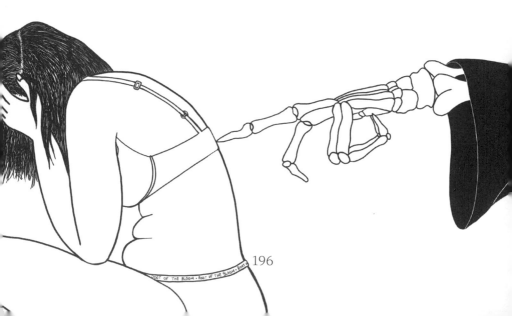

when nothing you need to do is completed,
you'll get up to go, but i'll keep you seated.

when you start to build hope and the future's bright,
i'll snuff out the sun and prolong the night.

no matter personal or financial success,
i'll crawl up your skin with the Reaper's caress.

when you're close to escaping but miss by a thread,
i'll be here waiting with a gun to your head.

# CHARGE

ok, but just so you know, that's going to be an extra 50 cents.

# CLICHÉS

is it "never give up on the one you love"
or "if you love them, let them go"
'cause these quotes are getting confusing
and, honestly, i just gotta know.
'cause they say "when it's right, it's easy"
but also that "relationships take a lot of work."
most would agree on the first one,
unless their loved one is a jerk.
they say that "time heals all wounds"
but also "absence makes the heart grow fonder."
how both sentiments could be true,
one truly has to ponder.
so should we have a lot in common,
or do opposites attract?
i suppose that depends on if you have similar interests
to the chick with the awesome rack.

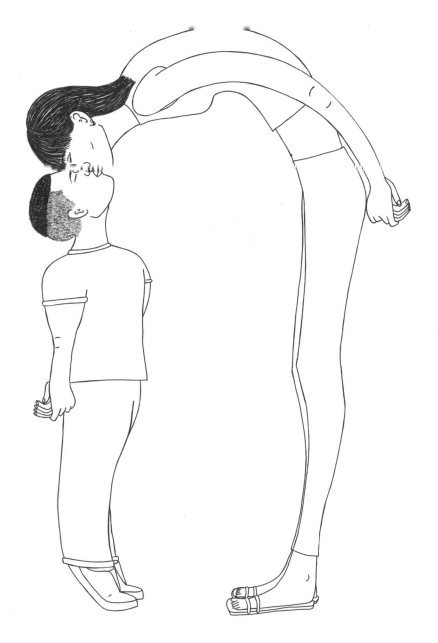

# WALLS

my neighbors have really loud sex, a lot of it.
i'm happy for them, i just wish she'd fake her orgasms
    a little more quietly.
i almost complained once, but then i realized:
if i can hear *them* having animalistic, passionate
    intercourse,
they can hear *me* watching 13 consecutive hours of
    f·r·i·e·n·d·s.


let bygones be bygones, i guess.

# DESPERATE

i like my men like i like my pizza.

i'm not very picky.

# ADVICE 13

ppl change i used to hate coconut & now i love coconut
so dont judge ppl on their past 2nd chances r real have
faith dont give up on ppl

# BOOBOO

you'll break my heart & glue it together;
i'll bruise your ego, then kiss it better.

you'll crush my soul & put a band-aid on it;
i'll kill your body, then i'll embalm it.

205

# HAUNTED

a ghost keeps on messing with me

in the most irritating ways.

he (she? it?) does all the typical ghosty things like

playing with the lights and messing with the doors.

sometimes my keys will disappear when i'm late

then reappear after i've already paid for an uber.

my lights will flicker when it's late and i'm alone,

but nothing ever happens when people are around.

sometimes stuff just falls off the walls!

seriously! it's some spooky stuff!

but he (it? they?) never does anything to hurt me.

unless you count the time he (they? she?) cut my power

while i was watching the finale of dexter, but

honestly even that ended up being more of a favor.

so i decided that my ghost isn't here to scare me,

he's (she's? it's?) just a lonely dude (gal? thing?)

that wants some company, a distraction.

so he (whatever) is welcome to

blow out my candle or lock me out anytime,

'cause i think we all understand what it's like

to be haunted by loneliness.

# ADVICE 6

dont believe everything u read i could write rn that i like tapioca but i hate tapioca it's the devils snack so ya dont believe everything u read unless u read that im cool u can believe that

# RAW

our love is like that chicken in the back of the fridge.
i know it's expired, i'm just not ready to throw it away.

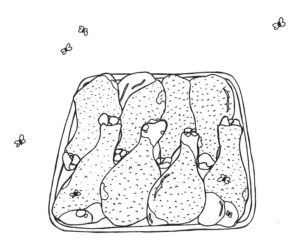

# TEACHER

the worst part about breakups is knowing that
some other girl will reap the benefits
of all the lessons i taught him.
everyone has to learn,
it just sucks being the teacher.

i hope you appreciate the way you two make up
after an evening of heated exchange.
i was his crash test dummy.

i hope you love the way he holds you
when you're feeling insecure.
i was the place holder.

i hope you notice how he listens when you speak
about the way he's upsetting you.
it took a lot of yelling to make his ears work.

i hope you enjoy that thing he does with his tongue,
and i'm not talking about the pretty things he says to
    you–
though i taught him that, too.


i hope you acknowledge the way he appreciates
the little things you do for him.
he didn't know what he had until he lost it.

that's right, i went through all the trouble
and some other girl will benefit from my hard work.
but, maybe, the next guy will have already learned
from the teacher before me.
maybe he'll have his degree in decency.
maybe he'll have graduated from boy to man.
and, probably, some other girl will have taught him how.

teachers truly have the toughest job.

# TUMBLE

you're fighting an uphill battle,
& you're falling fast.
as much as you'd like to bring me with you,
i'm not jill and you're not jack.

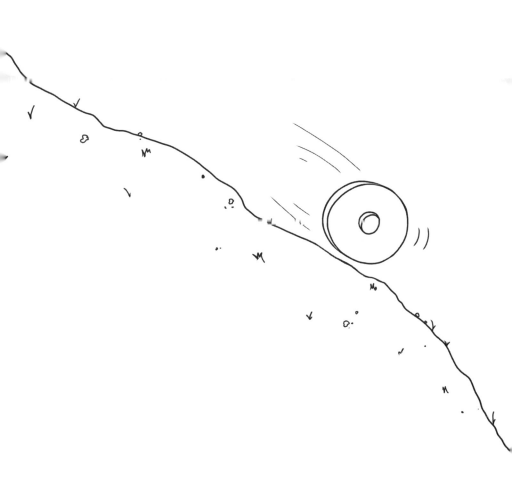

# GROWN UP

you've changed.

thank God, i was the
fucking worst.

# ARTIST

his alarm clock is the sound of your head hitting the
    pillow.
when your eyes shut, he opens his blinds.
it's time for you to rest after your hard day's work,
but his is just beginning.
after all, someone's got to produce the movies
you're going to watch all night.

> someone's got to make you fly
> across the orange and cloudy sky.
> someone's got to paint the picture
> of the guy who's a weirdly sexy mixture
> of your fifth-grade substitute english teacher
> and that one famous television preacher.
> he'll make you bold and unafraid
> to fearlessly take center stage
> and give the performance of a lifetime–
> all while you're tucked in tight at bedtime.

but art isn't always beautiful, it isn't always kind.
art is pain, art is fear, art is insecurity.
not all movies are romance or comedy.
some films are drama or horror,
some are psychological thrillers . . .

and the artist doesn't play favorites.

he makes you fly, but he'll let you fall
into an abyss where you'll have to crawl
through an obstacle course of bones and mud
to greet a vampire who wants your blood.
someone's got to sketch the monster
with venomous teeth and flea-ridden fur.
if you find you're naked in public, blame him;
he's the douche that will make you swim
through dismembered limbs and severed heads–
all while you're safe and sound in bed.

for every dream, there is a nightmare,
        and each night's sleep is a gamble.
so try and enjoy the show
        'cause either way, sleep is inevitable.

oh, and i forgot to mention,
sometimes he'll force you to make out with your cousin,
that fucking pervert.

# EXPIRED

i find people who suck me dry,
or maybe they find me.
i'll always lend a helping hand,
but for me there's no guarantee.
that is, of course, unless i have
something they might need.
looks like the price of loneliness
has an exchange rate of greed.
but i'll hang with peeps who take what they can
then vanish without a trace,
'cause i guess that being all used up
is better than going to waste.

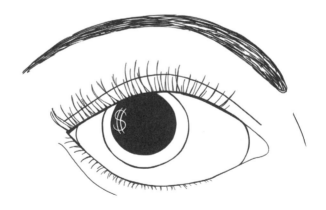

# WAR

every day is just
a battle between
am i too hungry to sleep
or too tired to eat

# BEAUTY

statistics show that beautiful people have it easier,
but i think in a lot of ways they have it way harder.
it sucks that they're constantly reminded of their looks
and honestly kind of personally punished,

because just like you can't help it that
you're smart
or good at guitar
or a born dancer
they can't help it that they're pretty.
i don't think it's fair that pretty people's
     accomplishments
are downplayed and chalked up to getting special
     treatment.
i can't tell you how many times i've heard someone
comment on a woman's success with
"must be nice to have big tits."
believe it or not, it's possible to have big tits
and also big dreams.
it's possible to have a great ass
and also a great work ethic.
it's possible to have a unique face
and also a unique sense of humor.
even people with jobs reliant on appearance
still work their perfect, round asses off to be better
than all the other beautiful unicorns in their field.
God graces everyone differently.
some people were graced with a high IQ.
some people were graced with musicality.
some people were graced with coordination.
some people were graced with beauty.

good for them.

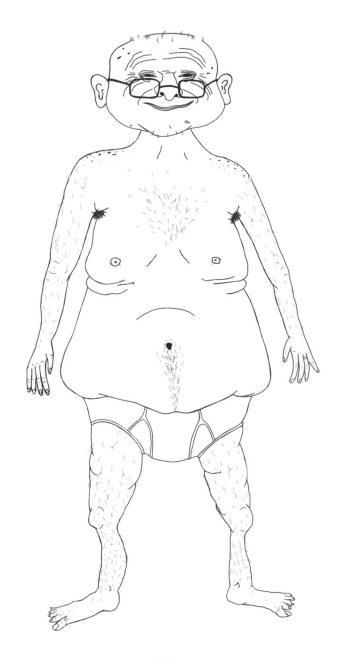

## ORDER

i saw a woman at a restaurant
choke on her meal and collapse.
i'll have what she's havin'.

## PRINCESS

real-life love is a lot like a fairy tale.
you gotta kiss a few frogs to find your prince,
and sometimes they give you warts.

# WRECK

"hop in," he said, "trust me, i'll drive."
then we went for the most magical ride.
he took me on a private VIP tour
and he showed me roads i'd never traveled before.

then he started to speed faster and faster.
"slow down!" i yelled, to avoid a disaster.
but he kept on rolling, quick and brash,
and before we knew it, there was a

C R A S H.

we survived, i'm alive;
but i'm covered in bruises and achy inside.
now i'm nervous in ways i wasn't before–
i'm fearful of cars and everything's sore.

sometimes there's no cut or gash
but you still feel the nagging bitch of whiplash.
some people want to rush to the future;
you can live in the fast lane, but the end comes sooner.

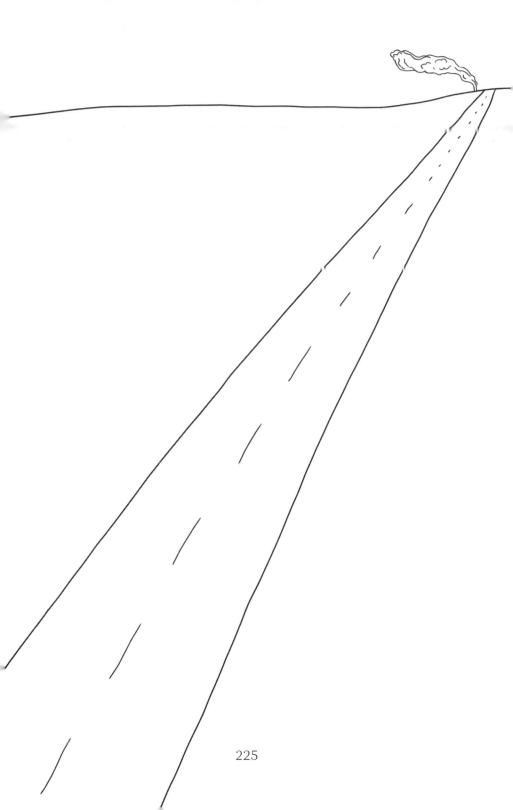

# OUCH

his hand in my hair
and his smile on my lips;
this is gonna hurt.

i bet you read that
and didn't even realize:
that's a haiku, bitch.

# EARTHQUAKE

the earth is shaking,
i am the epicenter
where the fault ruptures.

another haiku?
this is some middle school shit,
did i do this one right?

# PERFECT

you're the funniest person i know.
besides bob from work, that guy's a riot.

you're the kindest person i know.
well after my sister, she makes me pancakes when i
    stay over!

you're the best listener i know.
besides my cat, she never cuts me off.

you're the most trustworthy person i know.
besides father kevin, but that goes without saying.

you're the best-looking person i know.
in person, that is. have you seen some of these
    instagram models?!

you're the most talented person i know.
if i'm not counting myself. i mean, have you read this
    book?!

you're okay i guess.
i think we should see other people.

# SCOOCH

life isn't about "fitting in,"

   it's about finding people who move over.

# GROW

i've never understood "you've changed" as an insult.
if people didn't change, we wouldn't have the wheel
or refrigerators
or hd tv.
without change, we wouldn't have modern medicine
or technology
or froyo that tastes like birthday cake.
if people didn't change, we would still be wearing
    diapers.
we'd still be afraid of the monsters under our beds.
we'd still be doing that weird thing with our makeup
that we did in middle school that our sister tried to tell us
looked bad but we insisted that she was just jealous.
maybe that was just me.
but we wouldn't know the quadratic formula
or the periodic table of elements
or the dewey decimal system.
well, i guess that wouldn't really matter that much.
people would still think the earth was flat!
what? that's a thing again? huh.

the point is, change is learning. change is growth.
change is beautiful and powerful and necessary.
so please, tell me i changed, because as far as i'm
    concerned,
that's no insult.
that's the best compliment you could give me.
before i changed, i was sad
and insecure
and defeated.
before i changed, i felt small
and alone
and fearful.
before i grew up, i acted in a way that was brash
and defensive
and combative.
yes, i've changed.
thank you for noticing.

# IDENTITY

i'm the cockiest most insecure
confident self-conscious self-
assured anxious proud self-
loathing person i know.

# IDK

i dunno, yanno?

# FILLER

some of these poems were written because inspiration

struck,

others were written because i had a deadline and

needed

   to

     fill

       pages.

         can you guess which are

Which?

# DRINK

people are really weird about handing homeless people
    money.


"i'd rather buy them a meal," they say.
"they'll just spend it on booze," they say.
so what if they do?
it's not just alcohol they're drinking, it's an elixir.
it's not the liquor they're buying, it's the numbness.
food will make them full, but maybe they'd rather empty
    their minds,
if only for a few hours.
you like a drink after a "hard day at the office,"
i think this guy deserves one after his hard night on the
    street.
just give the guy a buck, would ya?

## GAMES

i don't know if i should play hard to get
or give in,
because i want you to miss me,
but i'm afraid that you won't.

# IMMORTALITY

what if, one day,
they make kids read this shit in english class.
it would only be way after i'm dead and gone, of course.
students would moan in agony at their poetry
     assignment.
i'd love to watch a teacher tell them what it "means"
and then quiz them on its "meaning."
i won't be around to correct them, of course.
then again, i guess poetry is open for interpretation.
regardless, it's gonna make for a lot of miserable pupils.
so many way cooler things you can be doing:
eating, if energy hasn't been shrunk to pill form by then;
tweeting, if that's still how people stroke their egos
     by then;
fucking, if that's still how people stroke each other
     by then.
sure bummed i won't be around to see it.


anyway, apologies in advance.

# ADVICE 12

growing up my mom always put the broken egg shells
back in the carton & it made me want to kill her in
her sleep but guess wut now im a grownup & i put
the egg shells back in the carton bc u know wut it's
convenient & distributes some of the weight & also
doesnt hurt any one so like dont give ur parents such a
hard time theyre not always wrong

# TROLL

if you're someone who hates without a cause,
someone who can't get their filthy paws
off their keyboard long enough to count to two—
i don't hate you back, i feel bad for you.
your venomed words can't break my callus;
i know there's pain behind your malice
'cause the thing you hate in everyone else
is probably the thing you hate most in yourself.

# CHASE

sometimes the person you want
will make you chase them.
so . . .
chase chase chase.
run run run.
burn lots of calories,
while you're at it, do some squats.
throw in some strength training.
sweat sweat sweat.
clean up your diet.
don't forget to stretch!
chase chase chase.
pretty soon you'll catch them!
and then
run run run
away.
you have better ways to spend your time
than with someone who made you
chase chase chase.
plus, now you're smokin' hot
and out of that douchebag's league.

go, you!

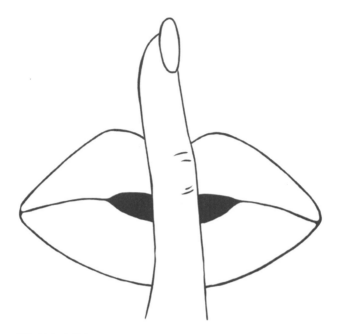

## SMALLTALK

hey, you.

person who needs to fill the silence.

yeah, you.

the one who would rather chat about the weather

than let a moment go without sound.

uh-huh, i'm looking at you.

the guy who has to hush the quiet.


what are you so afraid of hearing?

## KNOTS

your heart works harder than any other muscle.
it's got enough to worry about having the responsibility
of pumping blood through your entire body to deal with
the extra strain you put on it with all these high hopes
and romantic thoughts.
all i'm saying is i think it deserves a massage.

# PERSPECTIVE

i had a nightmare.
we drove off a highway.
a truck was coming straight for us
and we were headed for
certain death.

in our final moments,
i told you that i loved you.

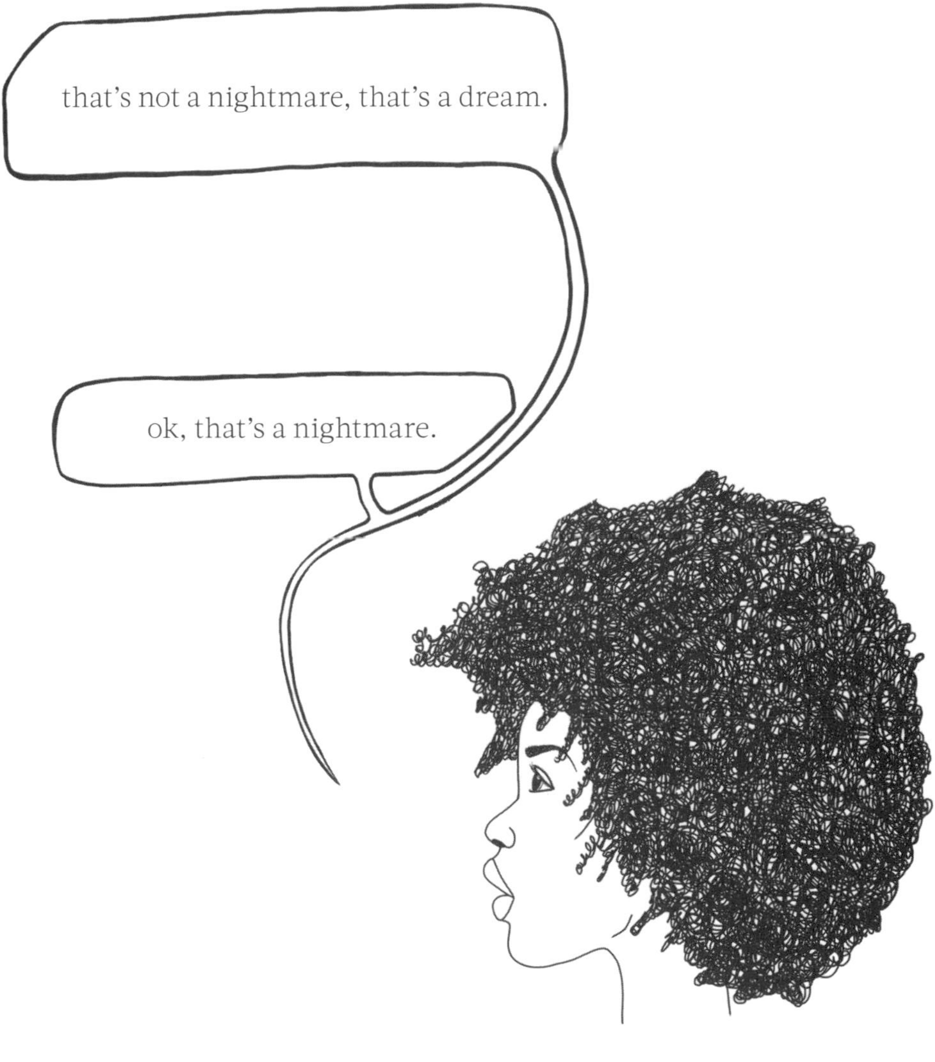
that's not a nightmare, that's a dream.
ok, that's a nightmare.

# STUFFED

you're an all-you-can-eat buffet.
everything i've ever craved,
and everything i didn't realize i wanted
until i got a taste.
you're chocolate sauce on pizza,
peanut butter on a cheeseburger,
an eclectic mix of things
that shouldn't belong together,
yet somehow perfectly do.
you satisfy my primal hunger
and satiate my sweet tooth.
            i always save room for dessert.

but i don't live here,
and i know that soon the waiters
will start to get antsy
and i'll have to go home.
until that moment comes,
i'll eat as much as i can,
sample every delicacy,
enjoy every morsel,
cherish every bite,
overindulge,
make myself absolutely sick
so that i can remember this feeling–
this full, uncomfortable, satisfied feeling–
when i wake up hungry.

# FIN

did you read this book cover to cover?
or did you skip around a bit?
did you share it with a friend or lover?
you better not have, make that bitch buy their own copy.
    i want a lamborghini.